What Kind of
Person
is Jesus?

VOLUME 1

Dr. Noel Enete
Dr. Denise Enete

we Demolish argument we captive
everythough + male it obedient
to Christ — Just the ons
against christ

WAVE
Study
Bible™

Published by Wave Study Bible, Inc.
www.WaveStudyBible.com
Edition 1.0.1

Scripture quotations noted **NIV** are taken from the *HOLY BIBLE, NEW INTERNATIONAL VERSION.*
Copyright 1973, 1978, and 1984 by International Bible Society. Used by permission of Zondervan Publishing
House. All rights reserved.

Scripture quotations noted **NASB** are taken from the *NEW AMERICAN STANDARD BIBLE,* Copyright 1960,
1962, 1963, 1968, 1971, 1972, 1973, 1975, 1977, by The Lockman Foundation. Used by permission.

The 4-*Step* Bible study strategy was adapted from Anne Graham Lotz's *Living a Life that is Blessed,* Copyright
1995 by AnGel Ministries.

Cover by graphic artist and jazz musician Dorothy Collins Wineman, *http://www.dotcollins.com.*

ISBN 978-0-9791595-1-0

Printed and bound in the United States of America

Table of Contents

Jesus
is a
strong leader

from Luke 8:22-25

What Kind of Person is Jesus?

1:
What Kind of Person is Jesus?

I [N] had never seen that kind of wetsuit—all red with one wide white stripe around the middle. But that is what one surfer began to wear surfing during the Christmas season. He also had the matching white-tipped red hat. The beach attracts its share of unusual characters and this middle aged guy would show up to surf at Christmas time in a Santa Claus wetsuit. He was a sight to behold but besides noticing him teaching some kids how to surf, I did not know much about him.

That all changed the Christmas of 1997. Our family had recently moved to the beach and John, our 15 year old son, was eager to catch some waves on the first day of his Christmas vacation. It was early in the morning. Nobody else from our family was surfing with him, but the waves were good and he was going for it.

After his first ride, he jumped off his board and landed on a broken bottle on the bottom of the ocean. It gashed his foot open. His foot was numb from the cold so he did not, at first, realize what had happened. As he paddled past the middle aged Santa Claus, the man drew John's attention to the gash.

Then this middle aged surfer helped John to the shore and brought him to his first aid kit. It turns out the man had a medical practice and taught surfing on the side. He cleaned John's wound, applied a temporary bandage and drove John to our house. I rushed John to the doctor, his injury required 14 stitches, and everything healed beautifully because of the prompt and expert attention he received from this kind surfer.

I did not know this surfer before the accident, but afterwards I felt a deep respect and thankfulness for him. What kind of person would leave a good surfing session, bandage a stranger's kid, and drive him home so he could get immediate medical attention?—a kind, compassionate, and giving individual. I came to know this person by watching him in action.

We come to know God the same way—by watching Him in action and asking ourselves, "What kind of person would do that?"

It may sound unusual at first, but God has a personality. That is *not* to say God is finite or limited in any way. Rather, it is to say we can have a personal relationship with Him. As we watch Him in action through the pages of the Bible, we get a sense for how He reacts to things and can begin to understand Him in the same kind of terms by which we understand our other friends.

There is no clearer way to see God in action than to watch Jesus in action because Jesus is God in the flesh. The way Jesus reacts to situations during His earthly ministry shows us how God reacts to them. Some things bring Jesus joy, other things anger Him. At times He is moved to compassion and at other times He is moved to warn.

As you watch Jesus in action, notice what He values and ask yourself, "What kind of person values that?" Notice what moves Him to compassion and ask yourself, "What kind of person is touched by that situation?" Identify what angers Him and ask yourself, "What kind of person is angered by that kind of thing?" These questions help you understand Jesus' personality so you can trust Him the way you trust a true friend.

God does not present Himself to us as merely a collection of spiritual absolutes. He presents Himself as an infinite and divine person that is touched by our feelings and can be known like we come to know a friend. Do not miss the opportunity to know God.

Organization of the Study Guide

This *Study Guide* takes you through several gospel passages that show Jesus in action and lets you decide for yourself what kind of person He is.

The format of this *Study Guide* encourages you to surface whatever you notice in the passages and respond to God accordingly. Then as you explore these passages, also be alert to notice what you can learn about what kind of person God is.

If you are not familiar with the *4-Step* method of studying the Bible, there is a section on page 8 that will explain what to write in the 4 panels associated with each passage.

A devotional commentary is also included after the passages that covers what you have just studied. This gives you something to compare your work against. The commentary also suggests a number of personality traits that can be learned about Jesus from the passages.

How To Fill In the Panels

Following each passage in this *Study Guide* are four panels that help you surface how God is speaking to you. Fill in the panels according to the instructions below.

1. Facts

In the *Facts* panel, make a list of the *Facts* you see in the passage. You don't have to list all the details. Just try and find the main points. You can use the same words as are in the passage. You will usually get somewhere around four to six *Facts*.

2. Lessons

In the *Lessons* panel, look over the list of facts and see what you can learn from the passage.

- Is there an example to follow?
- Is there a behavior to stop or start?
- Is there a comfort to accept?

Also, consider what you can learn about God from this passage? What does He value? What does He respond to? What pleases Him? You don't have to find a *Lesson* from every verse. Usually you will get one or two *Lessons* from a passage.

3. Challenges

In the *Challenges* panel, turn each *Lesson* you surfaced into a question that *Challenges* you. Listen for God to speak to you. He may not speak to you through every verse, but He will speak to you. You will normally get the same number of *Challenges* as *Lessons*.

4. Response

In the *Response* panel, consider what God is saying to you through this passage and decide how you will respond. Write out your *Response* as a two or three sentence prayer.

Be heartfelt and honest with God. If needed, put "training wheels" on your *Response:* "Lord help me to want this." Better to be honest and ask for help, than promise behavior you are not ready to keep.

5. Commentary

Now that you are clear on what you see in the passage, we give you the *Commentary* panel where we describe what we see in the passage. If you find something helpful in this panel, add it to your current understanding.

In this step you are comparing your study against that of an authority. If there are differences, do not automatically discard your idea. Rather, look at both concepts and see which makes the most sense to *you* and adopt that as your new understanding.

Example: Psalms 121

To get an idea how to fill in the panels, the following pages present *Psalms 121* studied using these panels. This is a guide to help you understand what kind of item goes in each panel.

More items are included in each panel than you would normally surface in the study of a passage. More are included to give you a better idea what goes in each panel.

Example Passage

Psalms 121:1 I lift up my eyes to the mountains; From where shall my help come?

Psalms 121:2 My help [comes] from the LORD, Who made heaven and earth.

Psalms 121:3 He will not allow your foot to slip; He who keeps you will not slumber.

Psalms 121:4 Behold, He Who keeps Israel Will neither slumber nor sleep.

Psalms 121:5 The LORD is your keeper; the LORD is your shade on your right hand;

Psalms 121:6 The sun will not smite you by day, Nor the moon by night.

Psalms 121:7 The LORD will protect you from all evil; He will keep your soul.

Psalms 121:8 The Lord will guard your going out and your coming in From this time forth and forever. (NASB)

1. Facts

List what you see in the passage

I look up and wonder where my help will come from.

My help comes from God who made heaven and earth

God won't let me fall because He is always watching,
He doesn't sleep

He keeps Israel and doesn't sleep or even slumber

The Lord keeps me and shades me at my right hand

I am not attacked by sun or moon

The Lord protects me from evil He is keeping my
soul safe

The Lord guards me now and forever

2. Lessons

Write down what you learn from this passage

There are times we know we need help beyond ourselves

Help comes from God Who created heaven and earth and is alert and ready to help

God is constantly watching, ready to catch me before I fall

He can be so attentive because He never sleep or slumbers

God "keeps" Israel; God "keeps" me. Keeping me means He observes me, guards me, takes care of me, maintains me, preserves me, retains me in His possession

3. Challenges

Turn the lessons into questions that challenge you

Am I humble enough to seek help when I need it?

Do I go to God for help, or something else?

Do I trust God to "keep" me?

Am I willing to learn what God considers "falling" instead of assuming falling means failure.

4. Response

Listen to what God is saying to you and write out your response

Lord, help me to be more aware of Your help and presence.

Help me see my relationship with You from Your perspective.

Jesus
does not play
with our emotions.

from Luke 8:22-29

2:
Passages

These passages take you through a study of Jesus in action. If you are unfamiliar with the *4-Step* method of studying the Bible, you will find a brief explanation on page 8. If you get stuck while studying a passage and want some help you can take a look at the *Answers* on page 75.

Done Oct 13

Luke 8:22 Now on one of [those] days Jesus and His disciples got into a boat, and He said to them, "Let us go over to the other side of the lake." So they launched out.

Luke 8:23 But as they were sailing along He fell asleep; and a fierce gale of wind descended on the lake, and they [began] to be swamped and to be in danger.

Luke 8:24 They came to Jesus and woke Him up, saying, "Master, Master, we are perishing!" And He got up and rebuked the wind and the surging waves, and they stopped, and it became calm.

Luke 8:25 And He said to them, "Where is your faith?" They were fearful and amazed, saying to one another, "Who then is this, that He commands even the winds and the water, and they obey Him?" (NASB)

together in a Boat
go to other side
halve

Jesus spending time with Disciple
not to be peactul

Jesus tired fell
asleep. Storm
Dangerous
swamped

The storm point
woke him up
Jesus spoke to
wind + water

master   afraid   performed a miracle

Not Trusting God   Didn't trust his capability
His power scared them
whatever gercorstances they didn't realise they
could call on God

I you love someone you calm their fears 1st

they were fisherman being tested

How do you ask in Faith
testing in a place where they know everything
about

would I be able to trust him in the face
of Danger

God Knows the future
Fully man He sleeps eats   He isn't panic
we can rest in God
He is a confident leader

the world has   Satan can't hurt God so he hurts us

as a man thinks of himself

1. Facts   so are you

List what you see in the passage

Jesus and His disciples got into a boat and Jesus said,
"Let's go across the lake."

Jesus is talking

whatever is true noble etc think about such things.

So you Don't get angry or Bolt

The world has definite philosophys
I. world   Just Do it   God   It is better to be patience than to conquer a situation

2. Power is everything   God   whoever wants to Be great among you will serve.
Be served/Not to serve

proverbs 1:2

3. I'm my own Boss   God   Every way a man's (servant?)

I Know Best
Do Not Conform any longer By this World then you will Be able to decern Gods ways

when you reject one of lifes assignments
you get bitter
when you ask the Lord you work all things for good

2. Lessons

Write down what you learn from this passage

When we follow Jesus He has a plan where He will
take us. Jesus didn't wander aimlessly around in this
passage. He knew where He wanted to go.

3. Challenges

Turn the lessons into questions that challenge you

Do I have confidence that if I follow Jesus He has a plan where He will lead me?

4. Response

Listen to what God is saying to you and write out your response

Commentary

Have you ever noticed that when you follow Jesus you don't get a detailed itinerary? The destination can be somewhat hazy: "Let's go across the lake." "Where exactly are we going?" "Why are we going across the lake?" "Who are we meeting across the lake?" "When will we be coming back?" "Do we need to take provisions for the night?" None of that is recorded, just, "Let's go across the lake."

When you have a strong leader who inspires confidence, you are willing to get in the boat without knowing all the details. Jesus is a strong leader. He doesn't wander aimlessly around. He knew where He wanted to go. He had a mission. He was not worried. He was relaxed enough to fall asleep allowing the others to take the helm. He didn't micromanage their every move. He wasn't barking out orders about speed and tacking. He let them be in charge of the trip. He was not wringing His Hands after He gave them the responsibility.

Jesus knew that problems bigger than we can manage will come up as we follow Him. The reason He was not worried and could sleep is because He is able to handle whatever comes up. That's why Christ's first question to His disciples was, "Where is your faith?" If they had taken Jesus at His Word, "Let's go to the other side of the lake," they would know He would get them there.

There will be danger for some as we follow Christ. Do we wait until we are desperate to seek Christ's help, or does our faith in Christ keep us from desperation?

Jesus is the kind of leader who puts His followers first. He was tired, but He got up and helped. He did not scold the disciples for interrupting His sleep. Instead, He responded

Commentary

to their fears immediately. He calmed the storm. He did not play with their emotions. Then He taught them what would have helped in their crisis—faith.

Jesus has ultimate control over His creation. His creation obeys His commands. Jesus "rebuked" the storm the way He "rebuked" demons. It is possible that Satan was trying to prevent Jesus from reaching the two demonized men on the other side of the lake. But Jesus just had to speak and the storm became calm. Satan is no match for Jesus. When there are earthquakes, fires, floods and tornados where is our faith? When we are frightened, Jesus responds immediately and says the solution is faith in Him.

Do I have confidence that if I follow Jesus He has a plan and will lead me? Am I willing to step out and get in the boat? God won't steer us if we stay put. But if we are willing to get in the boat, even if we get in the "wrong" boat, God can steer us in His preferred direction. God gives us a lot of freedom to choose to follow Him. He does not micromanage us and force us to follow Him. The more time we spend with Jesus in the boat, the more we will become like Him. If we are a worried leader now, He will help increase our faith so we will feel secure enough to let others take the helm. Because ultimately we know He is the one in charge.

Am I willing to follow Christ even when there is danger? Will my faith keep me focused on Him? Do I see how Christ will put me first? Do I see that He won't chastise me for my fear, but will help me both with the danger and with my faith. Do I see how Christ cares about my fears and won't play with my emotions? He did not tell the disciples their fear was silly. He asked them where their faith

Commentary

was. The danger was real. But, His power over the danger was also real.

Getting to know Jesus also helps us not fear His power. The disciples were amazed and afraid of Jesus' power over His creation. If they had understood His mission to die for them, they would not have feared His power, but felt secure in it.

What kind of person is Jesus?

- Jesus is a strong leader. He is confident and doesn't wring His Hands trying to micro-manage us.

- Jesus is the kind of person who when He says something, He is powerful enough to make it happen. Jesus said, "Let's go to the other side of the lake." If the disciples took Him at His Word they would not need to fear, they would know they were going to get to the other side.

- Jesus responds to our fears and then teaches us how to cope better next time.

- Jesus does not play with our emotions. He dealt with the storm immediately. He didn't chastise them first.

- Jesus has absolute power over His creation. He only needed to speak and the storm was calmed. Normally it takes hours for the waves to settle after a storm. Satan is no match for Jesus.

- Jesus let the disciples take the helm.

- Jesus uses His power to protect us.

Getting to
know Jesus
helps us not fear
His power.

from Luke 8:25

Mark 12:41 And He sat down opposite the treasury, and [began] observing how the people were putting money into the treasury; and many rich people were putting in large sums.

Mark 12:42 A poor widow came and put in two small copper coins, which amount to a cent.

Mark 12:43 Calling His disciples to Him, He said to them, "Truly I say to you, this poor widow put in more than all the contributors to the treasury;

Mark 12:44 for they all put in out of their surplus, but she, out of her poverty, put in all she owned, all she had to live on." (NASB)

1. Facts

Jesus sat so He could watch the people in the treasury.

2. Lessons

Jesus takes time to notice those who seem insignificant to the world.

3.   Challenges

Turn the lessons into questions that challenge you

Do I take time to notice those who seem insignificant in the world?

4.   Response

Listen to what God is saying to you and write out your response

Commentary

"Have you noticed that Jesus never seems in a hurry? He never gets flustered rushing around. In fact, He was criticized for not hurrying a time or two. Here is another example of Jesus taking His time. This time, Jesus shows us He cares about our giving.

Jesus sat down opposite the offering box and just watched the crowd put money in the box. He saw many rich people throwing large amounts into the box. That didn't move Him to comment. But, when a poor widow put in less than a penny, He saw the teachable moment.

He called for His disciple's attention and assured them what He was about to say was the truth. He needed to tell them it was the truth because otherwise, they might think He was kidding. He said the poor widow put in more than all the others. Huh? The others gave large amounts. This was a radical statement. Then He explained in God's economy giving all you have is more than giving out of your excess. The widow would probably not eat again until she earned more. The rich were unaffected by their gift.

Jesus just leveled the playing field. He is not looking for our money. If it were the amount of money, only the rich could give a lot to God. Rich or poor can "give the most" if they give sacrificially. Ultimate faith is giving sacrificially because you trust God, rather than your bank account, to be your security. There is freedom in not pinning your security to a penny. There is freedom in pinning your security to God.

We should take heart that Jesus takes time to notice the "insignificant" in the world. He uses a different measuring stick to measure significance. You don't need fame and for-

Commentary

tune to be important to Jesus. He is impressed by our faith. He supernaturally knew the widow's financial situation. He saw that her security was not pinned on her money.

Where is my security? Am I focused on getting fame and fortune or on giving sacrificially? God is so fair. We can all give sacrificially. We can all give "the most." Jesus knows all about our financial situation and approves of giving, even when we are poor. God's ideas are radical and we won't think of them ourselves. If we trust God with our money, we are trusting Him with our heart.

What kind of person is Jesus?

- Jesus cares about our giving because it reflects our trust in Him.

- Jesus is never flustered or in a hurry. He sits down and waits. He is confident He will accomplish what He has determined to do.

- Jesus takes time with His disciples to teach. He observes the offering box until the teachable moment.

- Jesus communicates carefully with His disciples. Because His teachings are radical, He warns them what He is about to say is the truth.

- Jesus is not money hungry. He did not comment on the large gifts of money. He commented on the large gift of faith. He wants us to focus on living a life of sacrificial giving because our security is with Him, not with our money.

- Jesus supernaturally knew the widow's financial situation.

- Jesus' teachings are liberating. We can all give "the most."

John 20:24 *But Thomas, one of the twelve, called Didymus, was not with them when Jesus came.*

John 20:25 *So the other disciples were saying to him, "We have seen the Lord!" But he said to them, "Unless I see in His hands the imprint of the nails, and put my finger into the place of the nails, and put my hand into His side, I will not believe."*

John 20:26 *After eight days His disciples were again inside, and Thomas with them. Jesus came, the doors having been shut, and stood in their midst and said, "Peace [be] with you."*

John 20:27 *Then He said to Thomas, "Reach here with your finger, and see My hands; and reach here your hand and put it into My side; and do not be unbelieving, but believing."*

John 20:28 *Thomas answered and said to Him, "My Lord and my God!"*

John 20:29 *Jesus said to him, "Because you have seen Me, have you believed? Blessed [are] they who did not see, and [yet] believed." (NASB)*

1. Facts

List what you see in the passage

Didymus

Thomas was not there when Jesus came   one of the 12

The other disciples saw Jesus

thomas need to see place of nails

multipule layers of proof

Thomas did not believe

after 8 Days   the Disciples were inside w/ Thomas

Jesus appear

Jesus spoke Peace they were freaked out

Jesus said put your fingers in hand in his wound

thomas: Jesus still had wound

Jesus wanted him to believe

He can read Thomas mind

Thomas acknowledge Jesus was his Lord

He didn't Defend himself He was humbled

Jesus identified him as a doubter he

encouraged him

Jesus asked Do you believe now

we are Blessed people that didn't have

to see to Believe & he rewards them

thomas didn't Believe all the other Disciples

whom he did not Know

Jesus is patient   Thomas is a show-me guy

2. Lessons

When we miss out on a blessing, there will be other
opportunities if we keep showing up where God wants
us to be.

when you find you do wrong
Do not Defend yourself

Listen to Holy spirit

8 Days - you have 2nd chances

Jesus Does not want to frighten us
But to say Peace be with you

Salvation thru Grace

3. Challenges

Turn the lessons into questions that challenge you

If I miss a blessing, do I realize that if I keep
showing up where God wants me to be, there
will be other opportunities for blessings?

Are you willing to be differente
keep trying to show up o learn

Am I willing to try to believe w/your
unbelief

4. Response

Listen to what God is saying to you and write out your response

Commentary

Have you ever heard, "You should have been here!! The waves were epic," "the fish was thissss big," or "the Spirit was so evident among us!" If so, you probably sigh and wonder why you had to miss out, or just figure they are exaggerating.

Thomas missed seeing Jesus and was probably disappointed, "Why did I have to miss this?" It is never fun to be the one who missed out. Maybe as an attempt to compensate, Thomas took another tact. He said, "I don't believe it." He was falling behind the others and this was his way to feel superior again. He was basically telling the others they were crazy and he didn't trust their account. Popular guy that Thomas.

But gracious Jesus gave him another chance. If we miss out on a blessing, Jesus provides other opportunities if we keep showing up.

Jesus made a point of showing Himself after His resurrection. He wanted the disciples to be eye witnesses so they could tell us about it. But, He also expected Thomas to believe the disciples' account, not needing visual evidence before he believed. We are in the same boat with Thomas. Jesus wants us to believe He is our Savior because it is true and because it was witnessed by many. Jesus does not want us to refuse to believe until we "get physical proof." He wants our relationship to be by faith.

In spite of what He wanted, Jesus cared about Thomas and his unbelief, so He gave Thomas a second chance. To Thomas's credit, he kept showing up. He did not walk away after his declaration of unbelief. Jesus allowed Thomas to get his

Commentary

"physical proof" while teaching everyone about the blessings of faith.

Notice how sensitive and kind-hearted Jesus is. He knew that miraculously appearing in the room without the use of a door might startle and frighten them. So, His first words to them were, "Peace be with you." He came in peace to teach and encourage. Thomas's response was quick in coming, "My Lord and my God." There are blessings in store for all who say by faith, "My Lord and my God."

What Kind of a Person is Jesus?

- Jesus is gracious. He gives second chances.

- Jesus does not get angry easily. Thomas announced his unbelief clearly, but Jesus came in peace.

- Jesus is comfortable with the title "My Lord and my God", but also humble enough to come in peace.

- Jesus is kind and sensitive. He does not want us to be afraid of Him. He wants us to believe Him.

Mark 14:32 *They came to a place named Gethsemane; and He said to His disciples, "Sit here until I have prayed."*

Mark 14:33 *And He took with Him Peter and James and John, and began to be very distressed and troubled.*

Mark 14:34 *And He said to them, "My soul is deeply grieved to the point of death; remain here and keep watch."*

Mark 14:35 *And He went a little beyond [them,] and fell to the ground and [began] to pray that if it were possible, the hour might pass Him by.*

Mark 14:36 *And He was saying, "Abba! Father! All things are possible for You; remove this cup from Me; yet not what I will, but what You will."*

Mark 14:37 *And He came and found them sleeping, and said to Peter, "Simon, are you asleep? Could you not keep watch for one hour?*

Mark 14:38 *"Keep watching and praying that you may not come into temptation; the spirit is willing, but the flesh is weak."*

Mark 14:39 *Again He went away and prayed, saying the same words.*

Mark 14:40 *And again He came and found them sleeping, for their eyes were very heavy; and they did not know what to answer Him.*

Mark 14:41 *And He came the third time, and said to them, "Are you still sleeping and resting? It is enough; the hour has come; behold, the Son of Man is being betrayed into the hands of sinners.*

Mark 14:42 *"Get up, let us be going; behold, the one who betrays Me is at hand!" (NASB)*

1. Facts

Jesus took the disciples to Gethsemane.

2. Lessons

Write down what you learn from this passage

Jesus will lead us where we need to go.

3. Challenges

Turn the lessons into questions that challenge you

Do I trust that God will lead me where I need
to go?

4. Response

Listen to what God is saying to you and write out your response

Commentary

Jesus had a specific plan and He gave the disciples specific directions. He led them to Gethsemane. He told the disciples to sit and wait while He prayed. He took Peter, James and John with Him as He went further into the garden. He knew He would need to go way beyond His comfort zone and He brought His three most dedicated disciples to watch and pray with Him.

Watching Jesus become troubled and distressed to the point of death put the disciples beyond their comfort zone as well. Jesus was sharing His most painful time with them in order to teach them and to teach us. He taught them how to "be real" and share their grief and sorrow. He was not trying to suffer alone. He allowed them to share in His sufferings and He was unashamed to fall to the ground and pray to His Father.

Jesus gave a wonderful approach to prayer. He came to His Father as a child. He called His Father what a child would call his father—"Abba" that is "Daddy." He acknowledged His Daddy's power to accomplish anything and He asked for what He wanted. Then He submitted to His Daddy's wisdom and plan by saying, "Not My will, but Your will."

Do I expect God's will to never cause trouble or grief? Am I being "real" with others when God's will is causing me deep trouble and grief? Am I willing to support others who are going through difficult times by staying with them and "watching?" Am I worried about appearances, or am I willing to throw myself to the ground to pray? Do I approach God as my Daddy while submitting to His authority?

When Jesus finished praying He saw His three most trusted disciples sleeping rather than watching and praying. At

Commentary

that point He did not belittle them, but He wanted them to take responsibility for their actions. So He asked Peter directly, "Are you sleeping?"

Then He challenged eter to stay awake and pray so he wouldn't fall into temptation. Earlier that evening, Peter had insisted that He would never deny the Lord. Jesus was preparing Peter for what was to come. He told Peter, "The spirit is willing, but the flesh is weak." He knew Peter was zealous in His spirit to do the right thing, but when push comes to shove, the flesh is weak.

Jesus' request was reasonable. It was not a selfish request. He was asking them to stay awake and pray in order that *they* would not fall into temptation. In Jesus' hour of greatest need, He was thinking of *their* welfare.

Jesus went and prayed three times for the same thing. It is good to repeat our requests to God. We are family and God wants us to come before Him as His children, acknowledging His power, asking for what we want, and surrendering the issue ultimately to His good judgement. God knows that doing His will is sometimes difficult and we will want another way out, like Jesus did. At that moment God wants us to demonstrate our trust in Him by staying connected in prayer, like Jesus did.

Am I willing to repeat my requests before God? Am I focused on my relationship with Him or just on getting what I want? Do I underestimate the need to stay alert and connected to God in stressful times to avoid temptation?

Three times the disciples could not stay awake. They seemed embarrassed as to why. Some use sleep as a way

Commentary

to avoid stress. Jesus was greatly stressed and they didn't know what to say or how to help. If they had taken Jesus at His Word, they would have known that just being there and praying was all that was needed. But they underestimated the value to Jesus of just being there with Him, and the value to themselves of resisting temptation through prayer. Instead, sleep was a way to avoid the reality of the situation and their feelings of helplessness.

Do I ever use sleep to escape being with others during a stressful time? Do I underestimate the value of just being with another person in their time of need?

Jesus knew when the hour of His betrayal had come. He was working His plan and announced the hour to His disciples. He told His disciples that He was going to be betrayed into the hands of sinners. He wanted them to be warned and to know what to expect.

Do I appreciate how much Jesus reveals will happen in the future so we are warned and know what to expect?

The disciples had let Jesus down. They had not watched and prayed with Him. Because of this, they were less prepared for the temptations that lay ahead. So, how did Jesus react to being let down? Did He say, "Forget it, you guys are useless to Me?" No, He said, "Get up, let us go. The one who betrays Me is at hand." Jesus did not forsake them because they had failed Him. They were still a team. Jesus called them to His side and continued to speak the truth clearly in order to help them.

Am I thankful that Jesus does not give up on me when I let Him down?

Commentary

Jesus knew who His betrayer was and announced his arrival. He cooperated with His betrayer. Otherwise Judas would not be able to betray Him.

Am I thankful Jesus was humble enough to cooperate with His betrayer? The God of the Universe was humble enough to give Himself into the hands of sinners?!

What kind of person is Jesus?

- Jesus is determined. He does not let personal suffering deter Him from doing God's will.

- Jesus is genuine. He shared His grief and distress with His disciples.

- Jesus is humble and willing to submit to God's authority.

- Jesus is gentle. He doesn't belittle us when we are wrong.

- Jesus is the kind of person who asks us to do what is in *our* best interest rather than what is in *His* best interest.

- Jesus is a team player. He did not give up on the disciples even though they had let Him down.

John 2:1 *On the third day there was a wedding in Cana of Galilee, and the mother of Jesus was there;*

John 2:2 *and both Jesus and His disciples were invited to the wedding.*

John 2:3 *When the wine ran out, the mother of Jesus said to Him, "They have no wine."*

John 2:4 *And Jesus said to her, "Woman, what does that have to do with us? My hour has not yet come."*

John 2:5 *His mother said to the servants, "Whatever He says to you, do it."*

John 2:6 *Now there were six stone waterpots set there for the Jewish custom of purification, containing twenty or thirty gallons each.*

John 2:7 *Jesus said to them, "Fill the waterpots with water." So they filled them up to the brim.*

John 2:8 *And He said to them, "Draw [some] out now and take it to the headwaiter." So they took it [to him.]*

John 2:9 *When the headwaiter tasted the water which had become wine, and did not know where it came from (but the servants who had drawn the water knew), the headwaiter called the bridegroom,*

John 2:10 *and said to him, "Every man serves the good wine first, and when [the people] have drunk freely, [then he serves] the poorer [wine;] [but] you have kept the good wine until now."*

John 2:11 *This beginning of [His] signs Jesus did in Cana of Galilee, and manifested His glory, and His disciples believed in Him. (NASB)*

1. Facts

List what you see in the passage

Jesus and His disciples were at the wedding.

2. Lessons

Write down what you learn from this passage

Jesus values weddings enough to take time to attend.

3. Challenges

Turn the lessons into questions that challenge you

Do I support and value weddings which are instituted by God?

4. Response

Listen to what God is saying to you and write out your response

Commentary

Jesus came to earth to complete a mission. Yet, He values weddings enough to take the time to attend. The institution of marriage is important to God. But, this particular wedding ran into an embarrassing snag. The bride and groom underestimated the amount of wine to have on hand and they ran out.

Enter Jesus' mother. She was the kind of guest who knew what was going on, and Who to turn to for help. She was straightforward and direct stating the problem to Jesus, "They have no wine." Jesus was straightforward and direct back, "What does that have to do with us? My hour has not yet come." You have to love His mother. She didn't argue with Jesus. She had faith in Him to solve the problem. She was persistent in her unselfish request. She had no idea how He would solve the problem, but she was not deterred when Jesus put her off. Her faith in Him remained. She directed the servants to defer to Jesus just as she was deferring to Him.

Jesus knew He was not "responsible" for the lack of wine ("What does that have to do with us?") The bride and groom had failed to provide enough. Even though it was not His responsibility, He responded to His mother's faith in Him. Jesus responds to faith. He had told His mother it was not His time, but her faith and persistence caused Him to act.

Jesus' mother rallied the servants to obey Jesus in whatever He asked. Jesus knew exactly what to do. He was able to take what they already had (water) to make what they lacked. That seems to be the formula to this day. Give Jesus what we have and He will use it miraculously. Fortunately, the servants were not lazy and obeyed Jesus completely.

Commentary

They did not fill the waterpots halfway. They filled them to the brim so Jesus could make the most wine possible.

Jesus respected the authority of the head waiter by deferring to Him regarding the wine. He did not try to steal the attention away from the head waiter, but gave His best and let the waiter be the judge. Jesus did not give adequate wine, He gave the best.

It is telling that Jesus' first miracle to show His glory only includes His disciples and lowly servants. Jesus is no respecter of persons. The servants must have gone home thrilled with the story of how they filled up the waterpots with water at Jesus' direction and when they drew it out it was wine. Being around Jesus is life-changing.

Jesus was a thoughtful guest. He turned the water into wine quietly. He did not strut around making sure everyone at the wedding knew what He had done. He did not wish to embarrass the bride and groom. Only His mother, the servants, and His disciples were aware. He was willing to help without a lot of credit. How many people would be satisfied to save a whole wedding from embarrassment when only the servants and disciples were aware of it?

What Kind of Person is Jesus?

- Jesus is aware of boundaries. He knows where His responsibilities begin and end. He does not force His will on us.

- Jesus is generous and willing to do more than His responsibilities when asked.

- Jesus is flexible. He started by saying His hour had not come, yet responded to His mother's request because of her faith in Him.

Commentary

- Jesus responds favorably to faith in Him.

- Jesus can take what we do have and are willing to give Him, to make what we lack.

- Jesus is a strong leader. He knows what to do to solve a problem, and can organize the task.

- Jesus respects human authority. He is God, yet He is willing to defer to the headwaiter to evaluate the wine.

- Jesus gives His best. The wine was the best, not just adequate.

- Jesus is no respecter of persons. He showed His glory, for the first time, to servants and disciples.

- Jesus is thoughtful. He did His miracle quietly so the wedding party's lack would not be a source of embarrassment to them.

- Jesus was willing to help without receiving a lot of credit.

Jesus is generous
and willing to do more
than is asked of Him.

from John 2:10

Matthew 14:14 When He went ashore, He saw a large crowd, and felt compassion for them and healed their sick.

Matthew 14:15 When it was evening, the disciples came to Him and said, "This place is desolate and the hour is already late; so send the crowds away, that they may go into the villages and buy food for themselves."

Matthew 14:16 But Jesus said to them, "They do not need to go away; you give them [something] to eat!"

Matthew 14:17 They said to Him, "We have here only five loaves and two fish."

Matthew 14:18 And He said, "Bring them here to Me."

Matthew 14:19 Ordering the people to sit down on the grass, He took the five loaves and the two fish, and looking up toward heaven, He blessed [the food,] and breaking the loaves He gave them to the disciples, and the disciples [gave them] to the crowds,

Matthew 14:20 and they all ate and were satisfied. They picked up what was left over of the broken pieces, twelve full baskets.

Matthew 14:21 There were about five thousand men who ate, besides women and children. (NASB)

1.   Facts

Jesus went ashore and saw a large crowd.

2. Lessons

People can find Jesus. He allows us to come to Him.

3.   Challenges

Turn the lessons into questions that challenge you

Am I seeking out Jesus to help me?

4.   Response

Listen to what God is saying to you and write out your response

Commentary

Jesus had heard earlier in the day that John the Baptist had been beheaded *(Matthew 14:10-13)*. The news caused Him to withdraw by boat to a secluded place by Himself. The people also heard the news and followed Him on foot around the lake to where He was.

Most of us would be irritated and grumble when we saw the crowd because we would want that time to regroup. But not Jesus. He saw their need and was not consumed with His own need. He was not too burdened to help those who were seeking Him.

He cared about them and healed their sick. He did not just give them spiritual advice. He gave them physical healing and physical food. He cares about disease and our physical bodies because we care about it so much. He knows what we need. Jesus helped in a very practical way.

But, sometimes, Jesus helps us by asking us to do what seems impossible. He told the disciples the crowd didn't need to go away to eat. "You give them something to eat," He said. Well, color the disciples dumbfounded. Earth to Jesus, "We only have five loaves and two fishes." "Bring them here to Me," was His reply. In that brief exchange Jesus gave the formula for doing God's will:

- Take God at His Word
  ("You feed them")

- Surface what you have to offer
  (five loaves and two fishes)

- Give what you have to God
  ("Bring them here to Me")

- Follow His instructions
  (He instructed the crowds to sit down)

Commentary

God can do the impossible with what we give Him but we might have to risk our lunch. And after all, it is our lunch and what are five loaves and two fishes going to do to address this problem any way? It is easy to just keep our lunch, eat it, and miss the miracle. Instead, if we look to God to meet our needs, we will be satisfied—twelve baskets full of leftovers was quite a return on the five loaves and two fishes.

What kind of person is Jesus?

- Jesus is not consumed by His own needs. He is never too burdened to have compassion for us and help us.

- Jesus helps those who seek Him out.

- Jesus gives practical help with our physical needs, not just spiritual teachings.

- Jesus cares about the health of our physical bodies.

- Sometimes Jesus challenges us to do what is impossible so we will look to Him.

- Jesus teaches by doing. He helps us see that if we take God at His Word, give Him what little we have, and follow His instructions, He can do the impossible.

- Jesus is generous. He provides more than we need.

Mark 11:15 Then they came to Jerusalem. And He entered the temple and began to drive out those who were buying and selling in the temple, and overturned the tables of the money changers and the seats of those who were selling doves;

Mark 11:16 and He would not permit anyone to carry merchandise through the temple.

Mark 11:17 And He [began] to teach and say to them, "Is it not written, 'MY HOUSE SHALL BE CALLED A HOUSE OF PRAYER FOR ALL THE NATIONS'? But you have made it a ROBBERS' DEN."

Mark 11:18 The chief priests and the scribes heard [this,] and [began] seeking how to destroy Him; for they were afraid of Him, for the whole crowd was astonished at His teaching. (NASB)

1. Facts

List what you see in the passage

Jesus entered the temple.

2. Lessons

Write down what you learn from this passage

Jesus was willing to take on sin in order to teach and correct.

3.   Challenges

Turn the lessons into questions that challenge you

Am I willing to face sin and take it on if need be?

4.   Response

Listen to what God is saying to you and write out your response

Commentary

Can you picture the setting? The Temple had become an ATM/market of sorts, something like a big swap meet. People were trying to make a buck selling oxen, sheep and doves, or changing money for a fee. Not a conducive setting for prayer and worship. It took away the "relationship with God" feeling and replaced it with a business. People would buy their sacrificial animal at the Temple at a higher price for the convenience of it. Buy the animal, offer it up, and be done—one stop shopping. The emphasis was on convenience, not on God. People did not need to take much time, or put much thought into it.

Enter Jesus. He had cleansed the Temple three years earlier with a whip *(John 2)*. But, things had become more corrupt than ever. He took on the sin because worship was being defeated and the worshippers were being exploited. Jesus had the power and presence to come in and gain control over the whole Temple. Can you imagine trying to gain control over a swap meet? He used a certain amount of force to gain control. He overturned tables and seats. He got their attention.

Then He began to teach the Scripture. He started by asking them, "Is it not written, 'My house shall be called a house of prayer for all the nations?' But you have made it a robbers' den." Jesus aligned Himself with God's Word. The people would recognize that Scripture had said the Temple was to be a house of prayer. They would see the discrepancy. They would identify that they had felt robbed by the vendors in the Temple. The crowd was amazed that one Man had the courage to come in and confront the sin.

Enter the chief priests and scribes. They heard everything and feared how quickly Jesus had identified the sin and

Commentary

brought the crowd to His point of view. The power and influence of the chief priests and scribes was being undermined and their income would soon dry up. Their solution was to plot to assassinate Him.

Jesus is so different from the chief priests and scribes. They exploited others for their own benefit. Jesus put His own safety at risk in order to help people worship.

Jesus was forceful about this sin because it exploited His people and made it hard for them to worship. Jesus did not deal forcefully with people about their individual sin. He did not take a whip to the woman caught in adultery. He did not overturn Simon's table when he was inhospitable and rude to Him or to the prostitute. Jesus is gentle and direct when teaching regular old sinners. He is forceful when confronting evil men who are exploiting others.

Could I be like Jesus?—Gentle and direct with regular old sinners, but forceful and confident when evil keeps people from coming to God? Am I willing, like Jesus, to align myself with Scripture when confronting evil?

What kind of a person is Jesus?

- Jesus is brave. He is willing to confront sin in order to teach and correct, even if it put His life in danger.

- Jesus is not weak or timid. He has power and presence. He gained control of the whole temple by using a measured amount of force.

- Once Jesus gained control, He was commanding enough to keep control, not allowing anyone to carry merchandise in the Temple.

Commentary

Compare what you see with what an authority sees

- Jesus gets angry when evil tries to exploit God's children and keep them from connecting with Him.

- Jesus is direct. He says clearly what God wants and how they are sinning.

- Jesus is forceful with an evil system that hinders His children from effectively coming to Him, but He is compassionate and direct with an individual's sin.

- Jesus is persuasive and engaging. The crowd is amazed at His bold teachings.

- Jesus is patient. He never stopped declaring God's will to His rebellious people, no matter how often they rejected it. He was willing to cleanse the Temple again.

Jesus put
His own safety at risk
in order to
help people worship.

from Mark 11:15

Passage 8—Luke 7:36-50

Luke 7:36 Now one of the Pharisees was requesting Him to dine with him, and He entered the Pharisee's house and reclined [at the table.]

Luke 7:37 And there was a woman in the city who was a sinner; and when she learned that He was reclining [at the table] in the Pharisee's house, she brought an alabaster vial of perfume,

Luke 7:38 and standing behind [Him] at His feet, weeping, she began to wet His feet with her tears, and kept wiping them with the hair of her head, and kissing His feet and anointing them with the perfume.

Luke 7:39 Now when the Pharisee who had invited Him saw this, he said to himself, "If this man were a prophet He would know who and what sort of person this woman is who is touching Him, that she is a sinner."

Luke 7:40 And Jesus answered him, "Simon, I have something to say to you." And he replied, "Say it, Teacher."

Luke 7:41 "A moneylender had two debtors: one owed five hundred denarii, and the other fifty.

Luke 7:42 "When they were unable to repay, he graciously forgave them both. So which of them will love him more?"

Luke 7:43 Simon answered and said, "I suppose the one whom he forgave more." And He said to him, "You have judged correctly."

Luke 7:44 Turning toward the woman, He said to Simon, "Do you see this woman? I entered your house; you gave Me no water for My feet, but she has wet My feet with her tears and wiped them with her hair.

Luke 7:45 "You gave Me no kiss; but she, since the time I came in, has not ceased to kiss My feet.

Luke 7:46 "You did not anoint My head with oil, but she anointed My feet with perfume.

Luke 7:47 "For this reason I say to you, her sins, which are many, have been forgiven, for she loved much; but he who is forgiven little, loves little."

Luke 7:48 Then He said to her, "Your sins have been forgiven."

Luke 7:49 Those who were reclining [at the table] with Him began to say to themselves, "Who is this [man] who even forgives sins?"

Luke 7:50 And He said to the woman, "Your faith has saved you; go in peace." (NASB)

1. Facts

A Pharisee invited Jesus to have dinner with him.

2. Lessons

Write down what you learn from this passage

Jesus was willing to go where He wasn't
respected in order to offer help.

3. Challenges

Turn the lessons into questions that challenge you

Am I willing to share God's love and help in a disrespectful environment?

4. Response

Listen to what God is saying to you and write out your response

Commentary

Have you ever felt like you were being "set-up?" Simeon the Pharisee asks Jesus to come to his home for dinner. Sounds hospitable. Sounds warm. But Simon's attitude and behavior aren't warm or hospitable. He is just looking for reasons to discredit Jesus.

When Jesus arrives he does not greet Him with the customary kiss. That would feel like a cold rejection. He does not provide water so Jesus can have His feet washed by a lowly servant. He is setting Jesus up to look dirty and dishonored. After guests are refreshed with the foot washing, it was customary to anoint their head with oil. Guests felt cared for, special and refreshed. Jesus received no anointing. He was mistreated and dishonored. He went to the table as a dishonored visitor. Jesus had not pushed His way into Simon's house. Simon had invited Jesus.

Many people would have left after such an insulting greeting. But not Jesus. He is humble and cares more about Simon and the others in his house, than about being treated with respect. He knew there was going to be a chance to teach and to forgive and so He stayed. Jesus is not a doormat though.

Enter the prostitute. She hears Jesus is having dinner at Simon's house and is bold enough to enter the house with her alabaster vial of perfume. She was humble enough to bow at His feet. She had faith and enough repentance to weep over His feet, using her hair to clean and dry them. Feet were the lowly part of the body, while hair was the glory. She used her glory on His lowly feet. She had enough love to repeatedly kiss His feet. She was thankful enough to extravagantly anoint His feet with the perfume.

Commentary

In stark contrast Simon, the "well-behaved" Pharisee, was mounting his case against Jesus. He thought to himself, "If Jesus were a prophet He would know she is a sinner and shun this woman." The Pharisee was blind to his own sinful behavior and clueless to what appropriate and loving behavior would look like.

Jesus knew Simon's unspoken thoughts to discredit Him. But Jesus taught him anyway. After Simon agreed to listen, Jesus told him the parable of the moneylender and two debtors. When Jesus asked him which one will love him more, Simon halfheartedly says, "I suppose the one he forgave more." By saying "I suppose," we get a hint of veiled hostility and resistance. But Jesus graciously validates his answer as correct.

What Jesus does next shows His care for both the critic and the sinner. He was willing to try to help His critic by spending time and energy teaching him. Simon was focused on the outward behavior of the prostitute. He missed how unloving his behavior as a host and as a Pharisee was. Jesus helped Simon see his unloving and unbelieving behavior in contrast to the prostitute's loving and believing actions. He taught Simon and those around that the amount of sin a person has was not the issue. God was willing to forgive much. The issue was faith. By pronouncing her sins forgiven He validates her and her faith and commends her for her love.

Once Jesus tells her, "Your sins are forgiven," the Pharisees start asking the right question, "Who is this who even forgives sin?" The obvious answer is God. Just in case there is any confusion Jesus clarifies to the woman, "Your faith has saved you." If that hostile audience

Commentary

thought their good works were going to save them, Jesus spells it out for them. They had a clear decision to make. Continue with pride and prejudice, oblivious to their own sin, or focus on Jesus Christ, God's Son, Who was offering forgiveness to all who believe.

God asks only that we believe in His saving work for us. He doesn't want us comparing ourselves with each other. That just leads to strife and uncertainty. He wants us to believe what He has done for us so we too can "go in peace" because our sins are forgiven.

Do you identify more with Simon or the "sinner?" Is your sin more inward or exposed? Simon's sin was more inward: unloving, prideful, inhospitable and resistant. The woman's sin was exposed. Everyone knew she was a prostitute. The solution is the same for both—recognize your sin, and have faith in Christ's payment for your sins. Jesus is gracious and reasonable. He was willing to come to a house where He would be mistreated so He could teach them all and reach a "sinner."

If I am unaware how much I need to be forgiven, I won't appreciate Christ's forgiveness of my sins. Once I am willing to recognize my own sin, faith in Christ is the answer, and love and appreciation for His forgiveness will follow. I might even dream up an extravagant expression of gratitude.

Christ will meet you where you are. He gently told Simon to recognize his proud and unbelieving heart so he could receive forgiveness. He did not lecture the woman on cleaning up her behavior. He validated her faith and forgave her. God responds to our faith in Him.

Commentary

Compare what you see with what an authority sees

What kind of a person is Jesus?

- Jesus is humble. He puts up with disrespect because there is an opportunity to teach and help.

- Jesus is not a doormat. He accomplished His goal to teach and forgive even in a hostile environment.

- Jesus was not embarrassed by the woman's display of emotion. He validated her in front of everyone.

- Jesus is confident and direct in His communication, but never mean.

- Jesus had compassion wanting the woman to know right then that her sins were forgiven and that she should go in peace.

- Jesus is bold and never intimidated. He might look like a dirty, dishonored guest, yet He still pronounces her sins forgiven.

- Jesus was willing to be criticized and misunderstood because helping and loving us is worth it to Him.

- Jesus loves us more than He needs our immediate respect.

- Jesus cares more about our faith than our sin.

- Jesus wants us to go in peace after we have sought His forgiveness.

Go in peace.

Jesus
is never
flustered or
in a hurry.

from Mark 12:41-44

Appendix A: Answers

More answers are given below than you are expected to find when you study the passages. Most people find four to six *Facts*, one or two *Lessons*, one or two *Challenges*, and one *Response* when they study a passage (see page 8). Extra answers are given here to help you better recognize *Facts*, *Lessons*, *Challenges*, and *Responses*.

Passage 1—Luke 8:22-25

Facts

- Jesus and His disciples got into a boat and Jesus said, "Let's go across the lake."
- Jesus fell asleep as they sailed.
- A violent windstorm came.
- The boat started filling up with water to the point of danger.
- The disciples woke up Jesus calling Him "Master" and telling Him, "We are about to die."
- Jesus got up.
- Jesus rebuked the wind and raging waves.
- The waves and wind became calm.
- Jesus asked them, "Where is your faith?"
- The disciples were afraid and amazed wondering who Jesus really was since the winds and water obeyed Him.

Lessons

- Sometimes we need to take Jesus at His word even if we are surrounded by the storms of life. If the disciples had taken Jesus at His word, they would have known they were going to get to the other side of the lake.
- Jesus wants our faith to be in Him, no matter what problems come up.
- Problems bigger than our ability to manage will come up as we follow Christ. The solution is our faith in Christ's ability to handle them.
- Jesus puts us before His own needs. He was tired, but He got up. He did not rebuke the disciples for interrupting His sleep. He taught them what would have been helpful for them in a crisis—faith.
- Satan is no match for Jesus. Satan might have been behind the storm trying to keep Jesus from getting to the demonized men at Gerasenes. Jesus was able to calm the storm by simply speaking a word.
- Jesus responds to our fears. He immediately calmed the storm. He did not play with their emotions.
- Jesus has ultimate control over His creation. His creation obeys His commands. When there are earthquakes, fires and floods, where is our faith?
- The disciples' lack of faith was more troubling to Jesus than the "dangerous" storm.

Challenges

- Am I taking God at His Word?
- Do I know that bigger problems than I can manage will come up as I follow Christ and that the solution is faith in Christ?
- Am I willing to follow Christ even when there is danger? Will my faith keep me focused on Him?
- Do I see how Christ will put me first? That He won't chastise me for being a bother to Him?
- Do I have faith that He will teach me what I need to increase my faith in order to manage a crisis?
- Do I rest in the idea that Satan is no match for God?
- Do I see how God cares about our fears? How He does not play with our emotions?
- Do I have faith that God has ultimate control over His creation?
- Where is my faith when there are earthquakes, fires, floods and tornados?
- When I am frightened, do I turn to God in faith?

Response

- Lord, please help me to trust Your leadership in my life. Please teach me how to follow You. Help me recognize the opportunities You give me and help me be brave enough to get in the boat with You.

Passage 2—Mark 12:41-44

Facts

- Jesus sat so He could watch the people in the treasury.
- Many rich people were putting in large amounts of money.
- A poor widow put in two copper coins worth less than a penny.
- Jesus called His disciples to come.
- He said, "I tell you the truth."
- He said, "This poor widow has put in more than all the others who gave."
- He said the rich gave out of their surplus, but she gave all she had to live on—all she owned.

Lessons

- Jesus takes time to notice those who seem insignificant to the world.
- God has a different measuring stick for significance.
- Jesus supernaturally knew the widow's financial situation.
- Jesus is impressed by sacrificial giving because it involves trust in Him.
- Jesus wants to teach us. He called His disciples to come to Him so He could teach them.
- In God's economy, the widow gave more even though she gave less money. God looks at the heart, faith, and trust.
- There is freedom in not pinning one's security to a penny. There is freedom in pinning your security to God.

Challenges

- Do I take time to notice those who seem insignificant in the world?
- Do I think God has no time for me because I seem insignificant in the large scheme of things?
- What is my measuring stick for significance?
- Do I realize Jesus knows all about my financial situation and approves of giving even when I'm poor?
- Do I see what a huge compliment it is to God for me to trust Him with my last penny?
- Do I see how sacrificial giving requires great trust in God?
- Am I coming to Jesus to be taught?
- Do I appreciate how fair God is? That we can all give sacrificially? That it is not about the amount of money?
- Am I giving "the most" for me?
- Am I trusting God with my money?
- Is my security squarely on God, or am I trusting my bank account?

Response

- Lord, thank You for noticing me. Please help me to be like You and take time to notice those who are "insignificant" by the world's standards, but significant by Yours. Please help me to be like them. Thank You that we can all contribute significantly if we obey Your teachings.

Passage 3—John 20:24-29

Facts

- Thomas, also called Didymus, was one of the twelve.
- Thomas was not there when Jesus came.
- The other disciples told him, "We have seen the Lord."
- Thomas replied unless I…
- …see the wounds from the nails in His hands,
- …put my finger into the wounds from the nails,
- …put my hand into His side,
- …I will never believe it.
- Eight days later Thomas was with the disciples in the house.
- The doors were shut.
- Jesus stood in their midst saying, "Peace to you."
- Then He said to Thomas…
- …Reach here with your finger and see My hands.
- …Reach here your hand and put it into My side.
- …Do not be unbelieving, but believing.
- Thomas answered, "My Lord and my God."
- Jesus said to him, "Because you have seen Me, have you believed? Blessed are they who did not see, and yet believed."

Lessons

- When we miss out on a blessing, there will be other opportunities if we keep showing up.

- Jesus wants us to believe He is our Savior, not because we have seen Him, but because it is true.

- Jesus wants us to believe what He says without having to have physical proof.

- Jesus does not want to scare us. His first words as He appeared were, "Peace to you."

- Jesus often accommodates our unbelief while teaching us.

- Seeing Jesus evokes a single response, "My Lord and my God."

- Jesus rewards belief in Him without "proof."

Challenges

- If I'm in the wrong place and miss a blessing, am I willing to keep showing up?

- Am I accepting God's Word by faith or am I skeptical, wanting proof of everything?

- Do I believe Jesus cares about my unbelief? Do I see how His Word is given to help my unbelief?

- Do I believe Jesus does not want to scare me?

- When I think about Jesus, is my first response, "My Lord and my God?"

- Am I anticipating the blessings, both now and later, for believing Christ is my Savior even though I can't see Him?

Response

- Lord, forgive me for missing out on Your blessings because I'm in the wrong place or because of unbelief. Thank You that You give so many opportunities for blessings if I keep walking with You.

Passage 4—Mark 14:32-42

Facts

- Jesus took the disciples to Gethsemane.

- Jesus told His disciples, "Sit here while I pray."

- Jesus took Peter, James, and John with Him.

- Jesus became very troubled and distressed.

- He told His disciples, "My soul is deeply grieved to the point of death; remain here and watch."

- Jesus went a little father and threw Himself on the ground.

- He prayed that if it were possible cause the hour to pass from Him.

- He said, "Abba Father, all things are possible for You; take this cup away from Me. Yet not what I will, but what You will."

- Jesus came and found them sleeping.

- He said to Peter, "Simon are you sleeping? Couldn't you stay awake for one hour?"

- He told them to stay awake and pray so they would not fall into temptation.

- He said the spirit is willing, but the flesh is weak.

- He went away again and prayed the same thing.

- He came back and found them sleeping.
- They could not keep their eyes open and did not know what to tell Him.
- Jesus came a third time and said…
- …Are you still sleeping and resting?
- …It is enough;
- …The hour has come
- …The Son of Man is being betrayed into the hands of sinners
- …Get up, let us go
- …Look, My betrayer is at hand.

Lessons

- Jesus will lead us where we need to go.
- Sometimes we have to step out of our comfort zone, like Jesus, to accomplish His plan.
- Sometimes doing God's will can be deeply stressful.
- When we are having deep stress, it is OK to be genuine. Jesus wasn't worried about how He looked. He went a little farther and threw Himself on the ground to pray.
- We should submit to God's authority like Jesus submitted to God the Father's authority calling Him, "Abba [Daddy] Father."
- Jesus asks us to take responsibility for our actions. He asked Peter to acknowledge that he was sleeping instead of watching.
- Jesus' requests are reasonable. He asked them to stay awake for one hour.
- Jesus has reasons for requesting things. The disciples needed to stay awake and pray so they would not fall into temptation.
- It is good to repeat our requests to God. Jesus gives us the model of repeating our prayers by coming to God multiple times.
- The disciples and Jesus were still a team even though they had let Him down. Jesus still wanted His disciples to come with Him.

Challenges

- Do I trust that God will lead me where I need to go?
- Am I willing to step out of my comfort zone to accomplish God's plan for my life?
- Do I expect God's will to never cause trouble and deep grief?
- Am I being "real" with my closest friends when God's will is causing me deep trouble and grief?
- Do I believe that God knows better than me and do I defer to His will?
- Do I take responsibility for my actions when I let someone down?
- Do I realize how reasonable Jesus' requests are, and that He has a reason behind His requests?
- When I have stressed filled days, am I willing to think of the welfare of others like Jesus did?
- Am I willing to repeat my requests before God? Am I focused on my relationship with Him, or just on getting what I want?
- Am I thankful that Jesus did not give up on His disciples or us, even though we let Him down?

Response

- Lord, thank You for having the love and courage to do your Father's will and die for me. Please help me to follow You and go where You lead me. I want Your will for my life.

Passage 5—John 2:1-11

Facts

- On the third day there was a wedding at Cana in Galilee.
- Jesus' mother was there.
- Jesus and His disciples were also invited.
- When the wine ran out, Jesus' mother told Him, "they have no wine left."
- Jesus replied, "Woman what does that have to do with us? My hour has not yet come."
- His mother said to the servants, "Whatever He says to you, do it."
- Jesus' mother was persistent. She was not deterred when Jesus put her off.
- There were six stone waterpots there for the Jewish custom of purification.
- They each contained 20 or 30 gallons.
- Jesus said to fill the waterpots with water.
- The servants obeyed Jesus completely.
- Jesus told them to draw out some and take it to the headwaiter.
- They took it to him.
- When the headwaiter tasted the water which had become wine, he did not know where it came from.
- The servants knew where the wine had come from.
- The headwaiter called for the bridegroom.
- The headwaiter said, "Every man serves the good wine first and after people have drunk freely serve the poorer wine. You have kept the good wine until now."
- The beginning of Jesus' miracles was done in Cana of Galilee.
- The miracle manifested His glory.
- His disciples believed in Him.

Lessons

- Jesus values weddings.
- We should have faith that Jesus can solve our problems.
- Jesus responds to faith. He told His mother it was not His time, but her faith and persistence caused Him to act.
- We should work with authority.
- We should give our best. Jesus did not give adequate wine. He gave them the best wine.
- We should respect everyone. Jesus included servants and His disciples to be part of His first miracle to show His glory.

Challenges

- Do I value weddings?
- Do I defer to Jesus Christ to solve my problems?

- Am I persistent believing in Jesus' ability to solve my problems?
- Do I appreciate how Jesus is willing to help me even when it is not His responsibility?
- Am I willing to give Jesus what I already have so He can use it to make what I lack?
- Am I trusting Jesus enough to defer to authority? Do I trust that Jesus controls the authority in my life?
- Am I thankful that Jesus gives me the best? Am I giving Him my all?
- Am I a respecter of people? Do I include people of no rank in my life?

Response

- Thank You Lord for the institution of marriage. Please help me to support and value what You have created.

Passage 6—Matthew 14:14-21

Facts

- Jesus went ashore and saw a large crowd.
- He felt compassion for them.
- He healed their sick.
- When it was evening the disciples came to Jesus.
- They told Him to send the crowds home because 1) the place was desolate without food and 2) the people could buy food for themselves if they went back to the villages.
- Jesus said they did not need to go away.
- Jesus told the disciples to give them something to eat.
- Disciples said we only have five loaves and two fish.
- Jesus said, "bring them to Me."
- Jesus ordered the people to sit down on the grass.
- Jesus took the five loaves and two fish and looked up toward heaven and blessed the food.
- He broke the loaves and gave them to the disciples.
- The disciples gave them to the crowds.
- They all ate and were satisfied.
- They picked up the leftovers and ended up with 12 baskets full.
- Not counting women and children, there were about 5,000 men who ate.

Lessons

- People can find Jesus. He allows us to come to Him.
- Jesus is never too burdened to help or respond to those seeking Him. Earlier that day, Jesus heard that John the Baptist had been murdered. He took off by boat to be by Himself, but the people followed Him on foot. His first response when He saw them was not irritation. His first response was compassion. He saw their need.
- Jesus cares about disease. He makes a point of healing sickness where ever He goes.
- Jesus sometimes asks us to do what seems impossible on our own. He said, "You give them something to eat." He allows us to find what we have to

offer (5 loaves and 2 fish). He instructs us to bring to Him what we have to offer. He does the impossible with our offering.

- Jesus likes order. He instructs the people to sit down so they could feed them more effectively.
- Jesus sets the example for asking God to bless our food. We look to God, not health food, for our life.
- When we look to God to meet our needs we will be satisfied.
- God's provision is generous and abundant.

Challenges

- Am I seeking out Jesus to fix my problems?
- Am I confident that Jesus has compassion on me, or am I worried He is too burdened or irritated with me and my problems?
- Do I believe that Jesus cares about disease?
- Do I walk away when Jesus asks me to do what seems impossible?
- Do I worry that the world is out of control or do I see the order in nature and in how Jesus dealt with the crowd of people?
- Am I relying on eating right alone to keep me healthy, or do I follow Christ's example and ask God to bless the food?
- Am I experiencing the satisfaction of how God provides?

Response

- Lord, thank You that You have made Yourself so available to me. Thank You that I can find You any time, day or night. Thank You for caring enough to be that available. Forgive me when I don't seek You out.

Passage 7—Mark 11:15-18

Facts

- They came to Jerusalem.
- Jesus entered the temple.
- Jesus began to drive out buyers and sellers in the temple.
- He overturned the tables of the money changers.
- He overturned the seats of people selling doves.
- He would not let anyone carry merchandise through the temple.
- He began to teach them asking a question and quoting Scripture, "Is it not written, 'My house shall be called a house of prayer for all the nations?' But you have made it a robbers' den."
- The chief priests and scribes heard Jesus.
- They began to plot how they would kill Him.
- They plot to kill Him because they were afraid of Him and because the whole crowd was astonished at His teaching.

Lessons

- Jesus was willing to take on sin in order to teach and correct.
- Jesus had the power and presence to come in and control the whole temple.
- Jesus used a certain amount of force to gain control.
- Jesus targeted those who were using the temple for financial gain.

- Jesus was able to enforce His ban on merchandise in the temple.
- After Jesus gained control He immediately began to teach them.
- Jesus teaches using Scripture.
- God guards His relationship with His own. Jesus was angry that the leaders were exploiting the people's worship and prayer to gain money. The people had to come to the temple and were "robbed" or required to spend money in order to pray and worship.
- Jesus was not afraid to confront sin even if it put His life in danger.
- Jesus did not forcefully confront an individual's sin. But when it came to exploiting God's meeting place with His people, He didn't want anyone getting in the way of coming to Him in prayer.

Challenges

- Am I willing to face sin and take it on?
- Do I see Jesus as powerful and commanding?
- Do I appreciate how Jesus could use a certain amount of force to gain control?
- Do I see how He targeted those who were using the temple for financial gain?
- Can I imagine how Jesus could enforce His ban on carrying merchandise through the temple?
- Do I appreciate that after Jesus gained control, He immediately began to teach the people?
- Do I use Scripture and questions when confronting evil?
- Do I see how serious it is when someone uses another person's relationship with God to exploit them?
- Do I appreciate how direct and clear Jesus is in His communications? Am I that direct and clear?
- Can I picture Jesus as commanding enough to be heard throughout the whole Temple?
- Am I willing to be that confident and "out there" taking a stand against sin that exploits someone's relationship with God?
- Am I too afraid to confront sin if it puts me in danger?
- Am I too forceful or direct when it is a person's personal sin?
- Do I see that the crowd would be amazed because Jesus has the courage to speak the truth that could liberate them?
- Can I picture Jesus as direct, powerful, commanding, clear, persuasive, brave and engaging?

Response

- Please help me draw from Your boldness and be willing to confront someone if they are exploiting people's relationship with You.

Passage 8—Luke 7:36-50

Facts

- A Pharisee invited Jesus to have dinner with him.
- Jesus went to his house and reclined at the table.
- A woman who was a sinner came with a jar of perfume.
- She stood behind Him at His feet, weeping.
- She wet His feet with her tears and wiped them with her hair.
- She kissed His feet and anointed them with the perfume.
- The Pharisee thought to himself, "If he were a prophet he would know she is a sinner and not let her touch him."
- Jesus answered his thought with an invitation to talk.
- Simon accepted His invitation.
- Jesus tells the parable of the moneylender who has 2 debtors and forgives both.
- Jesus asks Simon which debtor will love the moneylender more?
- Simon says the one forgiven the most.
- Jesus says he was right.
- Jesus specifies Simon's hospitality sins that evening.
- Jesus compares Simon's blindness to his sin to the woman's awareness of her sins.
- Jesus says the woman's awareness of her sins results in faith and greater love.
- Jesus forgives her sins.
- The others thought, "Who is this who even forgives sins?"
- Jesus said her faith saved her, not her love or behavior.

Lessons

- Sometimes we have to go where we aren't respected to offer help.
- We needn't be embarrassed when someone extravagantly loves Jesus.
- If we understood our sin we would have extravagant love for Christ.
- Jesus knows our thoughts.
- God loves sinners.
- Those who are forgiven the most appreciate and love the one who forgives them the most.
- God sticks up for the downtrodden sinner who has faith in Him.
- Pride gets in the way of recognizing our own sin.
- God meets us where we are. He validated the woman in front of the hostile group and told her that her sins were forgiven. He told her this before she had cleaned up her act.
- When our faith is in Christ for forgiveness, He wants us to go in peace.

Challenges

- Am I willing to share God's love and help in a disrespectful environment?
- Am I too embarrassed to show love for Christ in a hostile environment?
- Can I be comfortable to love Christ extravagantly or to be around someone who is loving Christ extravagantly?
- Am I comfortable that Christ knows my thoughts—that we are that close?

- Do I love sinners?
- Do I realize the magnitude of my sin in order to increase my love and appreciation for forgiveness?
- Do I stick up for the downtrodden sinners God loves?
- Is pride getting in the way of recognizing my own sin?
- Do I believe that God will meet me where I am? Am I willing to meet others where they are?
- Do I live in the peace of forgiveness?

Response

- Lord, please help me to be like You in hostile environments. May I be confident in my faith and Your message. Thank You for rewarding faith in You.

Appendix B: About the Authors

Dr. Noel Enete

Noel has a Bachelors from Baptist Bible College, a Th.M. from Dallas Theological Seminary in original language exegesis and a Doctor of Education specializing in Internet-based training systems. He has taught Bible and Theology for Dallas Bible College and has authored the *Wave Study Bible*® app for those with an iPhone, iPad, or iPod Touch.

Dr. Denise Enete

Denise has a Bachelors from Baptist Bible College and Masters course work at Dallas Theological Seminary. She also has a Masters and Doctor of Psychology and has had a private clinical psychology practice. Her specialty is integrating biblical truth with principles of good mental health. She has written a monthly column for a local paper on mental health topics and published a story in *Chicken Soup for the Bride's Soul*. They have been married since 1972 and have four adult children.

Contact

If you have suggestions or simply have benefited from this *Study Guide*, feel free to drop the authors an e-mail at the address below. Unfortunately, they will probably not be able to reply, but they would love to hear from you.

noel.enete@wavestudybible.com
denise.enete@wavestudybible.com
*(their last name is pronounced eee **NET**)*

Sometimes
Jesus helps us
by asking us to do
what seems impossible.

from Matthew 14:16